Aladdin

Illustrated by
Jaime Diaz Studios

Cover illustrated by
Sue DiCicco

Published by
Louis Weber, C.E.O.
Publications International, Ltd.
7373 North Cicero Avenue
Lincolnwood, Illinois 60712
Ground Floor, 59 Gloucester Place, London W1U 8JJ

Customer Service: customer_service@pilbooks.com

www.pilbooks.com

p i kids is a trademark of Publications International, Ltd.,
and is registered in the United States.
Look and Find is a trademark
of Publications International, Ltd.,
and is registered in the United States and Canada.

8 7 6 5 4 3 2 1

Manufactured in China.

ISBN: 978-1-4508-5628-7

 publications international, ltd.

Welcome to Agrabah, the home of Aladdin. Do not be fooled by his tattered clothes, for young Aladdin is destined to find a magic lamp. While his future is bright, right now the Sultan's guards are after him for stealing bread.

Can you find Aladdin and Abu before the guards do? Then locate these other Agrabah residents.

Aladdin

Abu

Princess Jasmine

The Sultan

Rasoul

Iago

Jafar

JUST TURBANS

TRÉS SHEIK

AGRABAH BROILED CHICKEN

SUNDIALS REPAIRED

PYRAMID TIMESHARING

VASE IS THE PLACE

Princess Jasmine's single days are numbered! Being the daughter of the Sultan, she must marry a prince by her birthday, and there are only three days left. Jasmine believes this law is unfair, but many eligible princes have gathered in the palace garden for the chance to win her affection.

Find these princes who don't seem to be Jasmine's type.

Prince
Ima Stinker

Prince
Havallama

Prince
Abracadabra

Prince
Jim Nastic

Prince
Chocolotts

Prince
Nick Nack

In the busy marketplace, Aladdin sees Princess Jasmine and is quite amazed by her beauty. Aladdin rescues Jasmine from an angry apple merchant. As they flee, Aladdin and Jasmine get separated in the crowd.

Help Aladdin find Jasmine! It will be difficult with these other Jasmine look-alikes around.

Jasmane

Jasmini

Jasthin

Jasmummy

Jasmirelda

Jasmonkey

Jasmineral

SUNDIALS REPAIRED

GRAND-FATHER SUNDIALS

ALARM CLOCKS

PYRAMID TIME-SHARING

CLEO'S HAREM DANCE STUDIO 6:00 AEROBICS

Delilah's Hair Salon

Samson's Gymnasium "DON'T HAVE SAND KICKED IN YOUR FACE!"

FRESH GOAT MILK IT'S NOT BAAAAAAAAAD!

FRESH FISH

TURBANS AND HEADDRESSES

HEADACHE TURBANS

URBAN TURBANS

TEN-GALLON TURBANS

Jafar, disguised as an old man, has tricked Aladdin into trusting him. Jafar promises the young man riches beyond belief if Aladdin will get the magic lamp from inside the Cave of Wonders. As they follow the scarab to the Cave of Wonders, a mirage appears, clouding their weary minds.

Help Aladdin locate the scarab and these other sandy things.

The scarab

Jafar in disguise

The Ghost of Gazeem

This sand box

The Sand Man

This sandpiper

This sandpaper

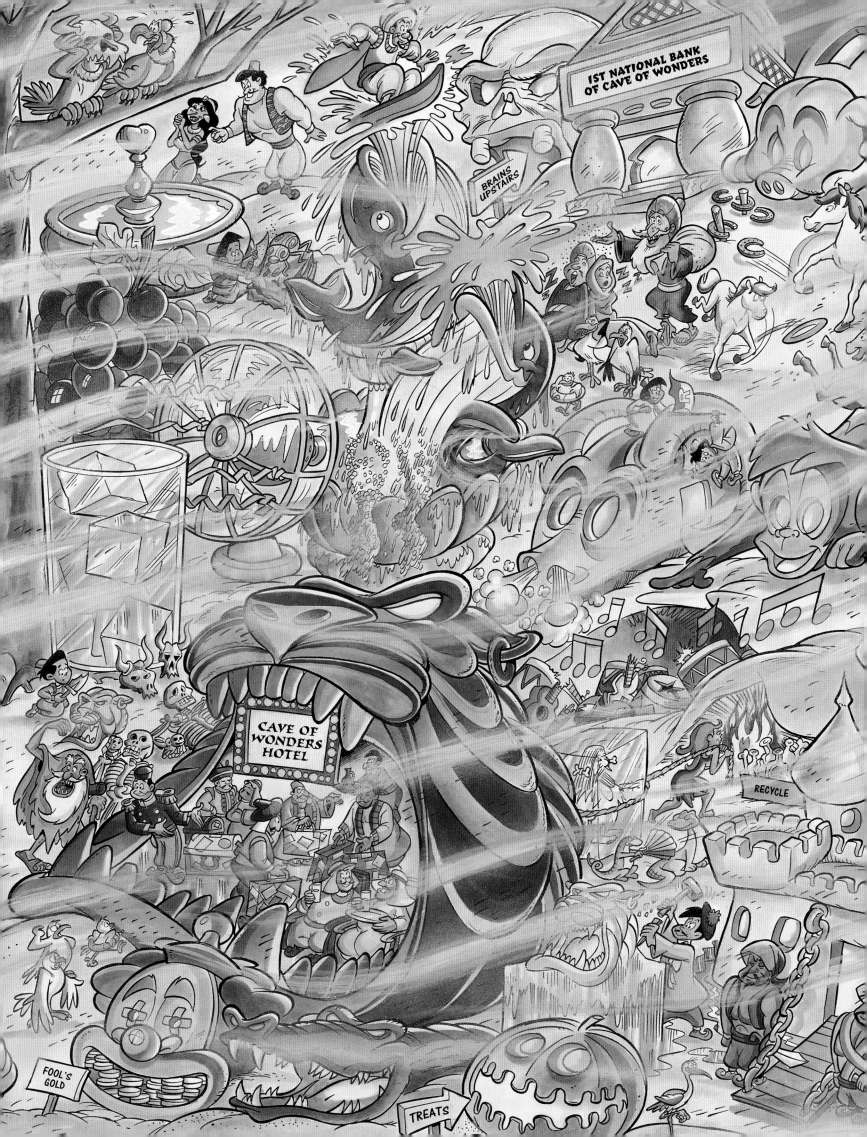

The Cave of Wonders contains riches beyond Aladdin's wildest dreams! Temptation is everywhere, but he must touch nothing except the magic lamp! Help Aladdin keep an eye on Abu and find the lamp and these other treasures.

Hi Ho Silver

Ruby Begonia

Baseball diamond

Diamond in the "ruff-ruff"

Pearly gate

Silver lining

Golden earring

Diamondback rattler

THE SPHINX FAMILY

OYSTERS
CHEAP

WRONG
LAMP

GOLDEN
FLEAS

MIDAS

JASMINE FAN CLUB

When Aladdin frees the Genie from the lamp, he discovers the Genie's many talents. One of these is granting wishes. Aladdin wishes to be a prince so that he can marry Princess Jasmine. The Genie turns him into Prince Ali and Abu into Aladdin's own elephant taxi. The city cheers as Ali parades through town.

Enjoy the parade and try to find these wonderful performers.

Queen for a Day

Juggles the Clown

Fire-eater

The human fountain

The human zero

Snake twirler

Snake charmer

Swami Salami

HE'S THE GREATEST

PRINCE ALI

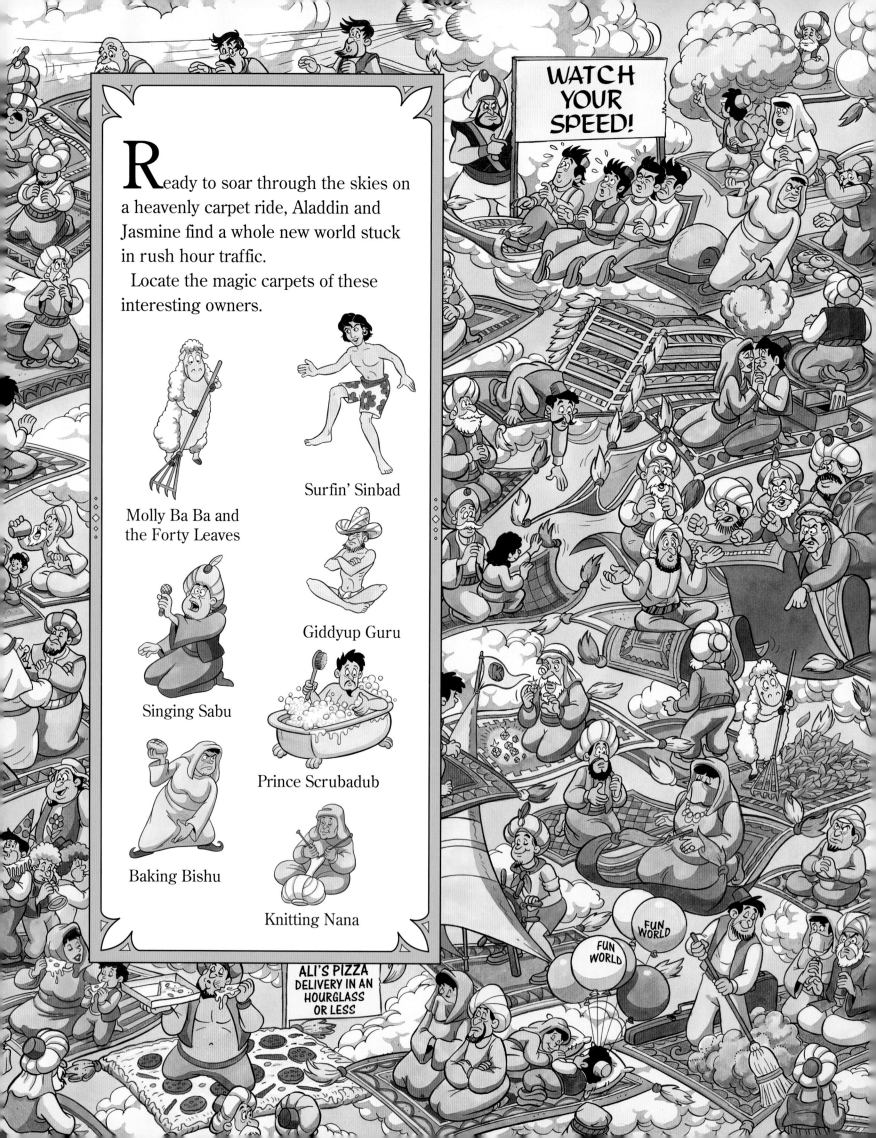

WATCH YOUR SPEED!

Ready to soar through the skies on a heavenly carpet ride, Aladdin and Jasmine find a whole new world stuck in rush hour traffic.

Locate the magic carpets of these interesting owners.

Molly Ba Ba and the Forty Leaves

Surfin' Sinbad

Singing Sabu

Giddyup Guru

Prince Scrubadub

Baking Bishu

Knitting Nana

ALI'S PIZZA DELIVERY IN AN HOURGLASS OR LESS

FUN WORLD

FUN WORLD

Leaping lamp oil! Iago has stolen Aladdin's lamp and now Jafar has become the most powerful sorcerer in the universe! Aladdin must find a way to trick Jafar and get back the lamp. It's a good thing Aladdin has plenty of friends, and Jafar has plenty of enemies.

Find the friends who are trying to help Aladdin.

Princess Jasmine

Royal chef

The Sultan

Carpet

Loyal subject

Abu

Free! After Aladdin cleverly tricks Jafar into becoming a prisoner inside of a lamp, the Genie is free to do whatever he wants. He decides to go to Fun World and enjoy doing… everything! And does he ever!

Find the Genie having fun as…

Junior Genie

Twist Genie

Squirt-Gunner Genie

Finally Free Genie

Inner Tube Genie

Ski Genie

GUESS YOUR WEIGHT

FERRIS DUNKER

BALLOONS $1 BLUE ONES FREE!

SHALLOW END

In the streets of Agrabah, Aladdin's athletic ability helps him to flee from the palace guards. Go back to find these other athletic things.

- ☐ Surfboard
- ☐ Golf club
- ☐ Soccer ball
- ☐ Bowling ball
- ☐ Basketball
- ☐ Fishing rod
- ☐ Tennis racket
- ☐ Hockey stick

In the palace garden, Jasmine found that the suitors didn't suit her, but she loved their horses. Find these other horse things.

- ☐ Horse scents
- ☐ Horse thief
- ☐ Horse fly
- ☐ Trojan horse
- ☐ Horse ride
- ☐ Horse and buggy

Aladdin fell in love with Jasmine in the marketplace. Go back and find these other falling things.

- ☐ Someone falling out of a window
- ☐ Someone falling into a well
- ☐ A falling star
- ☐ Someone falling off a camel
- ☐ Someone falling asleep
- ☐ Someone falling into a puddle

Searching the desert for the Cave of Wonders, you will find so much sand and so many caves. Go back to spot these caves and other crazy things.

- ☐ Mammoth Cave
- ☐ Cave of Fools
- ☐ Cave of Abu
- ☐ Sand dollars
- ☐ Caveman
- ☐ Sand witch
- ☐ Bat cave
- ☐ Sand crab